# A Scribble Where it Shouldn't

Paul Wennersberg Louhelen

illustrated by
Anton Kulakov

Now parents are always saying—
"Don't do this and don't do that!"
"Don't wear knickers on your head,
And please don't terrorize the cat!"

They tell you how you should behave
And, adversely, how you shouldn't.
But growing up is about trying new things
And doing what before we couldn't.

Now Luna was a cheeky girl,
who didn't always follow the rules,
And one night she did something naughty,
That she should never have done at all...
She drew a scribble where it shouldn't be,
Right on her bedroom wall!

Then she nodded off to sleep.

Oh what a silly thing to do,
But Luna didn't have a clue,
About scribbles where they shouldn't
And the things they get up to.

For a scribble is a mischievous thing
That comes alive at night,
And the last thing that you need
Is to wake up with a fright.

Now the scribble where it shouldn't
Felt a little out of place,
So he hopped right off the wall
And landed right on Luna's face.

Luna, she stirred a little,
But luckily she didn't wake.

So the scribble tip-toed off the bed
And surveyed his new place.

There was something shiny in the corner
Which caught the scribbles eye.
He ran over and found a mirror
And let out an excited cry!

For there was another scribble looking right back at him!

Now, scribbles are very friendly things,
So the first scribble waved hello,
Then helped the second out the mirror,
Oh what a crazy show!

Then the two conspired,
As scribbles often do,
And they came up with a plan, Oh no!
What were they going to do?

The scribbles found the crayons
And decided to draw some more.
And where once there were only two scribbles,
Now suddenly there were four.

They partied in the dolls house;
Then drove around in Barbie's car;
Then built a tower out of wooden blocks
To look out at the stars.

Then one swung on the door handle
And the door swung open wide.
And where before they were stuck in the bedroom,
Now they were free to roam outside.

Everyone was still asleep,
Except for a startled mouse,
As the scribbles where they shouldn't...
Went where they shouldn't- through the house!

And these scribbles went on scribbling—
Drawing this and drawing that.
They drew mustaches on the pictures
And silly glasses on the cat.

They scribbled on the walls,
And all over Mum's antiques,
Only stopping from the scribbling
For a quick game of hide and seek.

How many scribbles can you see?

The rooms were covered from top to bottom,
Even on the windows and the drapes.
Oh what was Luna going to say
When Mummy and Daddy were awake.

The scribble party went on all night,
And as you can probably guess,
When Luna's parents awoke the next morning,
Let's just say they weren't impressed.

Luna awoke and came downstairs,
And was more than a bit surprised...
For there were scribbles almost everywhere.
She couldn't believe her eyes.

Now Luna, she apologised
For she had drawn on the wall.
But she only remembered scribbling the one scribble...
She hadn't drawn them all.

Her parents gave her a **big** hug and smiled.

"It's okay", they said,
"We know it wasn't just you".
"Remember, we were also young once,
And we drew scribbles too!"

"Now how about we clean up all this mess,
Then maybe when we're done,
We can and go out and have ice-cream for breakfast
And go and have some fun!"

So remember, a scribble is a mischievous thing
That comes alive at night,
And the very last thing that you need
Is to give your parents a fright.

So if you want to draw a scribble
Then do it where you should,
For a scribble where it shouldn't
Only gets up to no good.

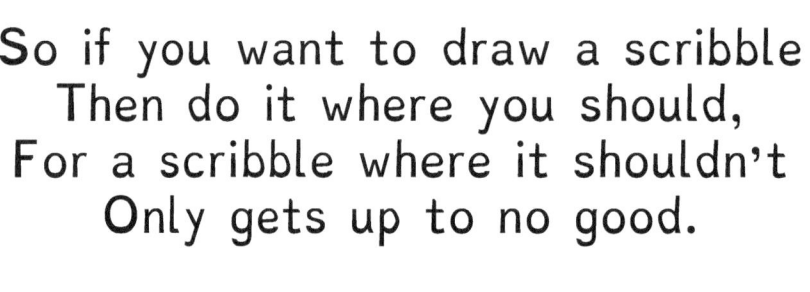

© 2022 Paul Wennersberg-Løvholen

No part of this book may be used or reproduced by any means, graphic, electronic, or mechanical, including photocopying, recording, taping, or by any information storage retrieval system without the written permission of the publisher except by reviewers, who may quote brief passages in a review.

*Text by Paul Wennersberg-Løvholen*
*Cover and illustrations by Anton Kulakov*

ISBN: 978-82-93748-25-0 (Hardback)
ISBN: 978-82-93748-26-7 (Paperback)
ISBN: 978-82-93748-27-4 (Kindle)
ISBN: 978-82-93748-28-1 (Ebook)

Published by Paul's Books, Eidsberg, Norway
fb.me/superfartypants

Also available from this author:

CPSIA information can be obtained
at www.ICGtesting.com
Printed in the USA
LVHW070349230322
714081LV00002B/201